The
Essential
Handbook
of
Prospecting

FOR NETWORK MARKETERS

Never Be Afraid of Prospecting Ever Again!

Jonathan Yap
Foreword by Tom "Big Al" Schreiter

The Essential Handbook of Prospecting for Network Marketers
© 2020 by Jonathan Yap

Published by Jonathan Yap

CONTENTS

Preface v

Foreword. 1

    Prospecting is scary. 3

    The real problem. 5

The Basics. 9

    The power of words. 11

    What business are we in? 15

    Case studies on then human mind. 21

    Getting prospects to pay attention. 27

    The survival program. 31

    The busybody program. 35

    I am just curious... 39

The Formula. 43

    A simple formula that works. 45

    Step #1: Building instant rapport. 49

    Let's get even better at building rapport. 57

    Step #2: Icebreakers. 65

    Step #3: Collecting decisions. 69

    Step #4: Presentation. (Part 1) 75

    Step #4: Presentation. (Part 2) 85

    Step #4: Presentation. (Part 3) 93

    Step #5: Call to action. 99

Putting Everything Together. 105

    Let's review. 107

    More examples. 113

    Is it really that easy? 123

    The rest is up to you. 125

About the Author 127

PREFACE

Before we begin, here are some quick questions:

- Are you able to create prospects whenever you want to?
- Do you have the ability to turn people into eager prospects within moments of meeting them?
- Is this a skill set you currently possess?

If you answered "no" to these questions, then you are reading the right book.

Just imagine what life would be like if you no longer had to chase prospects and beg them to buy your products or join your business, only to be left feeling humiliated and rejected when they stop returning your calls or replying to your messages.

In this book, we are going to talk about a specific set of skills that you can use to flip the situation around. You will have prospects chasing after you, eager to give you their money and longing to join you.

This is a set of skills that almost anyone can learn. It doesn't matter if you are an introvert or extrovert, rich or broke, and it even doesn't matter if you are good-looking or not.

So, if you are ready, come with me, and let's begin our journey and discover the secrets to creating eager prospects on-demand.

FOREWORD

By Tom "Big Al" Schreiter

PROSPECTING IS SCARY.

Prospecting is an essential part of building a successful network marketing business. However, for most distributors, prospecting is one of their biggest fears.

When you meet prospects:

- Do you feel nervous?
- Do you feel insecure and a lack of self-confidence?
- Are you afraid of rejection?

Well, if you are just starting out in network marketing or if you have been around for a while but have not had a high level of success in prospecting, then it would not be a surprise if your answer to any of the above questions is, "Yes."

Now, if you answered "yes," understand that these feelings are normal. If you have these feelings, it means you are human. And there is nothing wrong with being human.

As humans, if we have not learnt the skills of a certain task, then it would be entirely natural for us to feel uneasy or even scared when we are trying to perform that task. Prospecting is no exception. Once we learn and practice the skills of prospecting rejection-free, our fears of prospecting will naturally fade away and be replaced with confidence.

Wait, I have to learn new skills?

The bad news is, yes, just like any other profession in life, network marketing requires us to possess a specific set of skills. However, the good news for us is that we can learn new skills. Just think about it. When we were born, we did not know how to walk, but we learnt.

And what about smartphones? At some point in our lives, we had to learn how to use a smartphone.

So, just like we learnt how to walk and use a smartphone, we can learn the skills to become effective at prospecting. And through practice, we will remove our fears, increase our success, and build up our confidence in the process.

Practice brings improvement.

Don't be discouraged if, after learning the skills in this book, your first few attempts at prospecting seem difficult. The more we practice, the more we improve and the easier it gets.

Here is a good story to illustrate this point. Imagine a child learning to write. At first, it will be difficult. But through practice, it becomes easier and easier for the child.

It is the same when it comes to prospecting. So, keep in mind that it will become easier through practise. And in time, you will become more successful.

THE REAL PROBLEM.

One of my favourite questions to ask network marketers is, "What seems to be the biggest problem you face in building your network marketing business?"

I have heard many answers over the years, but the two most common replies are:

- I don't have anybody to talk to about my business or product.
- I can't find any good prospects.

Have you heard these before?

If you find yourself currently facing these two problems as well, don't worry. I used to be stuck in the very same shoes as you when I first got started in network marketing.

Here is a short story.

Let's imagine that I am a new distributor and my sister has a graduation party for my nephew. So, I go to the party and I walk through the door. The first thing that happens is my aunt grabs me, pinches my cheek and says, "Hey, you! Haven't seen you for a long time. So, what are you doing nowadays?"

Now, because my sponsor did not teach me exactly what to say, I don't know how to answer my aunt's question. So, I make something up on the spot and say, "Well, I am kind of in my own business now. What I do is buy products at wholesale and sell them at retail. Now, these products are really special, so you can't get them in stores. You need to know somebody that will sponsor you in. So, I am kind of building my very own distribution network now."

Pretty soon, my aunt says as she backs away from me, "You sell drugs!"

Now, I am thinking to myself, "That did not go too well. I'll need some food to comfort myself."

So, I head over to the buffet table and start stuffing my face with food, when out of nowhere, an old friend comes up and slaps me on the back and says, "Hey, you! Haven't seen you for a long time. So, what are you doing nowadays?"

At this point, my face is turning red, I start sweating and thinking, "I don't want my friend to think I am selling drugs, so, I'd better try the company approach."

So, I turn to my friend and say, "I am with The Wonderful Company. The headquarters is located in The Wonderful City. Founded in the year of 1991 by Mr Wonderful himself, who is a wonderful family man, and he has several families to prove it. We've got a wonderful product and a wonderful commission plan. In fact, our commission plan is so wonderful that it has created many top-earners. Come, let me show you some pictures of our wonderful leaders posing next to their wonderful sports cars and wonderful mansions. Everything is just wonderful, wonderful, wonderful!"

Now, my friend is thinking, "You've joined a cult! And if I joined with you, I would sound just as stupid as you."

So, I think to myself, "I have had enough humiliation and embarrassment for one party. I am out of here!"

So, I run out of the party, hop in my car, head down to the mall, and dive into the first restaurant I see. The waiter hands me the menu and we start talking. After a bit of small talk, the waiter looks at me and says, "Nice chatting with you. By the way, what do you do for a living?"

I freeze and just stare at him blankly. Pretty soon, he says, "I know! You are a mime, aren't you? You know, one of those people who don't talk."

And that is the day most distributors have when they first get started. They don't know what to say and do. It is embarrassing and humiliating. And when they get enough rejection, what are they going to do?

Quit!

Now, are we starting to see where the problem lies?

It is not that we don't have anyone to talk to or that we can't find any good prospects.

In fact, the opposite is true. We meet potential prospects in our daily lives. The real problem is that we don't know exactly what to say to these people when we meet them.

So, the solution is simple. We need to be able to talk to these people in a way that bypasses their mental defense programs so that we speak directly to the decision-making part of their minds.

But now that we know where the real problem lies, we can start to fix it by learning the necessary skills that will turn us into prospecting superstars.

THE BASICS

By Jonathan Yap

THE POWER OF WORDS.

I remember when I first got started in network marketing, I was taught to make a list of my family and friends. So that's what I did. I made a list of about two hundred people and then I started talking to each of them.

To cut the long story short, nobody joined my business and my brother was the only person out of all my family and friends that bought a product. And he only did so after I agreed to never talk to him about my opportunity again. In other words, he bought a product to shut me up.

But that was not the worst part. The worst part was that everyone else told me, "No."

Then it got even worse.

I did not give up after everyone I knew told me, "No."

Why? Because I was motivated. After all, I had been to a company training where we held hands as we sang motivational songs, screamed positive affirmations till we lost our voices, hugged each other while we cried, and patted one another on the back to give encouragement.

So, motivated and unwilling to quit, I went out to make new friends.

This is where it gets worse. The new friends I made hated what I said just as much as my old friends. And, as you've probably already guessed, all my new friends also told me, "No."

After 46 months and talking to over 700 people about my business, I finally learnt that finding new prospects was not my problem.

If I talked to over 700 people and everyone told me no, what was the problem?

Was everyone I talked to unmotivated losers that did not want anything more in their lives? Or was I just unlucky 700 times in a row?

No, of course not. When we think about it, we realise that the problem was me. Because of what I said to my prospects, they made a decision not to join me in my business or be my customer.

The solution.

After 46 months of absolute failure, I made a decision to figure out exactly what I need to say when I meet a prospect. And since nobody I knew seemed to have the answers I was looking for, I decided that I would learn by trial and error.

So, I started writing down different words and phrases I could use, and then I would go out and look for people to talk to and "try out" the words and phrases I had scripted out.

Was it difficult? Did I have a tough time?

Yes, but it was worth it.

Through my series of experiments, I discovered a couple of key things about human behaviour.

Key #1: Humans are creatures of reaction.

This means that whenever someone tells me "no," they are simply reacting to the things I say and do. For example, if I go out and approach a total stranger on the streets, and I wave and say hello, what would happen?

Well, most people would say hello back to me while giving me a puzzled look.

Why? The puzzled look is because I am a total stranger and they can't remember where we may have met before. However, they still say hello back to me because that is what we do. When someone says hello, we react by saying it back.

Now, what if I did something different? What would happen if instead of saying hello, I shouted at that person?

What might happen?

Would that stranger wave at me and say hello? No, definitely not!

So, why the difference in reaction? It was because of what I said and did which caused a different reaction from the very same person.

Key #2: People love people who talk about them.

The mistake I made was that every time I talked to a prospect, I was focused on talking about the features and benefits of my company, products, and opportunity. In short, I was just focused on pushing my agenda. The prospects felt that I did not care about them and was just trying to sell them something.

When I shifted the focus of my conversations from talking all about my company and products to listening to my prospects, they felt that I cared about them and they started to open up and tell me about the problems they were facing in their lives and why I should let them join me in my business.

Just imagine, all I did was change a few words I used, and I had flipped the situation around.

What happened next?

After 46 months of absolute failure, I started making money.

And all I had to do was to change the words I use. That was the missing link! People had not been turning **me** down; they were turning down how I presented my business to them.

And seven months after that, I was making a full-time income.

In conclusion.

Humans are creatures of reaction and our prospects are no exception.

So, if everyone we talk to is telling us "no" when we present to them, then what we have to do is look at ourselves. When we can change what we say, we will get different results.

And the good news is that changing to better words is entirely within our control.

WHAT BUSINESS ARE WE IN?

As we already know from the last chapter, different words and phrases will get different reactions from our prospects. Some words and phrases will put them on the alert and raise their mental defenses, while others will bypass their defense programs and send our message directly to the decision-making part of their minds. This brings us to our next essential point.

What business are we really in?

When we ask this question, most network marketers would give answers such as:

- Nutrition business.
- Skincare business.
- Healthy weight-loss business.
- Travel business.

The list goes on and on.

But are we really in any of those businesses?

Let me give you the short answer: No.

If you ask me, as network marketers, we are not in any of those businesses. Our companies are in the nutrition, skincare, weight loss, or travel businesses. But we don't work in the company. We are not their employees. The company doesn't need us to develop the website, design brochures, do product research and development, package the skincare cream into jars, and more.

Our network marketing company needs us to do the one thing that they cannot do. They need us to get people to make "yes" decisions to be customers and buy the products, or to be distributors and build a business with the company.

This means that we are in the decision-making business.

Sceptical?

Well, think about it this way. We can cut pictures and paste them on our vision boards, set our goals, sing motivational songs, chant affirmations, go out and look for prospects, hand out flyers, hand out samples, or even invite prospects to attend our opportunity meetings.

These are all great activities to do, but unless our prospects decide to be our customers or our business partners, we are not going to make any money.

We have to get our prospects to make "yes" decisions to do business with us. If not, we don't get paid.

Now that we are clear that we are in the decision-making business, we can focus on what is important. We don't have to stress about memorising the flipchart presentation, re-designing the brochure, or even laminating the compensation plan chart.

We can do all those things and more later. For right now, our immediate task at hand is to get our prospects to make "yes" decisions.

So, how do we get our prospects to make decisions?

Now that we know we are in the decision-collecting business, naturally, the next step is to find out how people make decisions.

I find this topic fascinating. There is no doubt that decision-making is an essential human behaviour. In fact, we make countless decisions every day. For example, on a daily basis, we need to decide what to eat, where to go, what to buy or not to buy, and the list goes on.

If we want to make money in network marketing, we need to find out how people make decisions. To be more exact, we need to find out how our prospects make decisions to buy our products, take advantage of our services, or join our business.

Now, I've got some good news and some bad news.

The bad news is that most of us never learnt how people make decisions. Furthermore, when it comes to a topic as complex as decision-making, we can't learn everything in one day.

On the other hand, the good news is that I am about to give you a crash course on how people make decisions.

To be able to guide prospects into making decisions, we must first understand what our prospects are thinking when they meet us.

When we take a look into the minds of our prospects, we will see that there are five basic questions that everybody will mentally go through when they encounter us. The five questions are:

Question 1: Who are you?

When we come into contact with someone, our minds automatically try to piece together any pre-existing information we have on that person. This is natural and just the way the human mind works because we have these survival programs that are deep-rooted in our subconscious minds.

So, our prospects, just like everyone else, are going to judge us the moment they come into contact with us. But don't worry too much.

Although having an outstanding personal brand helps, it is not necessary. So, if you are working on building up your personal brand, continue to do so. That will help you in the long run. For now, we can learn some really cool skills to build instant trust with our prospects, so they believe the good things we say even if we are not celebrities with outstanding personal brands.

Question 2: Can I trust you?

We can have the best product in the world, and we can have the best compensation plan in the history of the world, but if our prospects do not trust and believe us, it is game over before we even begin our presentation.

The difference between amateurs and professionals is that professionals know that when we talk about our business or product, the first few seconds are crucial. In those first few seconds, our prospects are going to either trust and believe the good things we say or put up walls of distrust and disbelief and not believe a single word we say. As professionals, we need to learn exactly how to manage these first few seconds and build instant trust and rapport with our prospects.

Question 3: Am I interested in what you are saying?

There is an old saying that the person who can capture and hold attention is the person who can effectively influence human behaviour.

Now, that may be true, but here lies the problem. We live in a world of too much information. Every moment of every day, we are being bombarded with tons upon tons of information. Due to this constant bombardment, our minds subconsciously narrow down and get us to focus on what is important to us. This is how the human mind works and our prospects' minds are no different.

So, as you can see, grabbing our prospects' attention and getting them to lean in and listen to what we have to say is a very competitive sport. Not only that, oftentimes, we only have mere seconds to grab that attention. Yes, our prospects will decide if they want to pay attention to us, or not, in a matter of seconds.

That is harsh, I know. But that is just how the human mind works.

Question 4: Do I want it or not?

Now, this is going to seem very weird to many of you, but here goes.

Our prospects are going to make their final decision if they want to buy or join before they have all the information. I know this may sound weird, but don't worry, we will have some case studies in the next chapter to show us how this works exactly.

Now, this can either be good news or bad news for us.

If we are amateurs and do not know how to handle the first 15 seconds when we talk to a prospect, then we will just have to suffer when our prospects don't show up to our meetings or come up with one objection after another.

The good news is that if we are professionals and we can handle this initial 15 seconds when we first talk to our prospects, then the rest of the conversation will be easier and our prospects will be listening to our presentation, without walls of disbelief, and looking for reasons to join instead of reasons not to join.

Question 5: Yeah, I want this product or opportunity. Can you give me some information, so I feel better about this?

This is where we can show the various products we have and talk about the opportunity in our fact-filled and detail-rich presentation.

What does this mean?

This means that our prospects will decide if they want to do business with us or not before they even see our presentation!

Is this fair? Of course not. But this is how the human mind works.

Do you find it hard to believe?

Most people find it hard to believe that prospects make their final decision before presentations. In the next chapter, we will take a look at how quickly decisions happen in the minds of our prospects.

Are you ready for some case studies?

CASE STUDIES ON THE HUMAN MIND.

In this chapter, we are going to look into some case studies which would reveal to us how the human mind makes decisions.

Are you ready?

Case study #1: Let's say we are hungry, so we go into a restaurant to eat. We look through the menu and we decide to have the chicken. Do we worry if the chicken lived a happy life before it was killed? Do we ask if the chicken farm that produced the chicken was debt-free? Do we think about whether the farmer was a wonderful family man?

No! We decided that we would order the chicken without a long presentation full of facts.

Case study #2: How about when we are on a video-streaming website and browsing around? How many seconds before we decide if we want to watch a particular video or not?

Well, most people do it within five seconds. Wow! In just a few seconds, we decided whether or not to watch the video. Did we need a full presentation with all the information about the video? No!

Case study #3: Have we ever received a telephone call from a telemarketer? How many seconds into the telephone call before we make our final decision? The truth is, most times, we make a "no" decision before the telemarketer finishes the first sentence.

We made a final decision before the presentation even started.

Here is an interesting question. If we are doing this to telemarketers, don't you think our prospects will do the same to us?

Case study #4: When we go shopping at the supermarket, what do we do? We grab a shopping basket and start walking. We come to the fruit section. There right in front of us are the apples. Do we check to see if they have a company video telling us about the apple farm? Do we stop to do a background check on the apple farmer? Do we ask if the apple farm is listed on the stock exchange?

No, definitely not. We make an instant decision to either buy the apples or bypass the apples.

Can you imagine if we had to stop and consider every single item in the supermarket? We would die of starvation before our shopping was done.

Case study #5: What about shoe shopping? There is a shoe store that has over three hundred different designs on display. A lady walks into the store and takes a look around. She doesn't see anything that she likes. She walks out within seconds.

What just happened?

Three hundred "no" decisions in a matter of seconds. She made three hundred instant "no" decisions without a single presentation on any of the designs. She was not shown a flipchart explaining the benefits of the leather or that the shoes are produced using a patented process that nobody else has.

Case study #6: Imagine someone comes up to us and says, "I have an aeroplane, but I don't know how to pilot it. I have never taken a flying lesson in my life. But it is okay. Let's all get on board this plane, fly off, and I will figure out how to pilot this plane along the way."

Are you in? No, of course not!

How quickly was our decision made? Well, if you are like most people, you would have made your final decision in a second.

Why? Because we have a program in our minds that says, "I don't want to die!"

So, due to our survival program, we made that immediate decision before we heard the details. We did not wait for him to tell us that he had watched a video online about how to pilot planes and that he had a 0.3% success rate.

Case study #7: What about relationships? Have we ever entered a relationship without having all the information first?

Ouch! Okay, that last one might be a little sensitive for some people.

But are we starting to see a trend?

We can see from our case studies that we humans make decisions almost instantly, **BEFORE** our presentation and not after.

So, what does this all mean?

When we are out there talking to prospects, what we do in the first 30 seconds is everything. In this first 30 seconds, our prospects' minds will go through the following:

Step #1: "Who are you?"

Step #2: "Can I trust you?"

Step #3: "Are you interesting?"

Step #4: "Do I want to do business with you or not?"

Yes, our prospects are going to decide if they want to do business with us or not in 30 seconds! That is how fast it happens.

Only after we take care of **Step #4**, then, and only then, can we move on to our presentation which happens at **Step #5**.

Step #5: "If I want it, give me the information."

This is the step where we talk about our products or opportunity.

This could include:

- Name of our company.
- Benefits of our products.
- How much our products cost.
- How to make money with our opportunity.
- Different levels of entry.
- The training and support our team will provide.

So, as we can see, the first 30 seconds when we talk to our prospects is extremely important because that is when they will make their decision.

If we want to be successful at network marketing, we need to learn how to handle this initial 30 seconds well. This is a key difference between an amateur and a professional.

What if they make a "no" decision?

If a prospect makes a "no" decision in the first 30 seconds, then we are done.

There is no need to torture the prospect with a three-hour-long presentation of facts and figures. We don't have to keep calling the prospect endlessly. Neither do we need to irritate the prospect by sending hundreds of text messages.

If the prospect made a decision not to do business with us, let's take a hint and stop stalking and harassing the prospect. Our time would be better spent if we move on and talk to prospects who want to do business with us.

Don't we have to follow up?

Yes, because their circumstances might change in the future, so following up with prospects is a good idea. If you look back, I never said not to follow up. What I said was to not be irritating and annoying by harassing our prospects endlessly.

There is a big difference between follow-up and harassment.

However, follow-up is not the main purpose of this book. This book is about getting "yes" decisions from our prospects. There are many books and trainings available if you want to learn how to follow up without being creepy, irritating, and annoying.

For now, let's get back to learning how to get "yes" decisions.

In conclusion.

As network marketing professionals, we must realize that our prospects are not going to make their decisions based on the company, the company founder, the products, the patents, the research and development, or the compensation plan.

Prospects are going to base their decisions on exactly what we say and do in the first 30 seconds when we introduce our business or products to them.

Wait, is this fair?

Well, I don't think this is fair and I am pretty sure most people reading this would agree with me. But this is simply how it works.

Our prospects make final decisions quickly.

So, let's focus on getting good at managing the first few seconds when we talk to our prospects about our business. When we can manage these first few seconds well, we not only make prospecting easier, we flip the situation around and make it unfair to our advantage!

Think about it. If we know how to get the final "yes" decision before our presentation:

1. We don't have to worry about coming across as a sleazy salesperson.

2. We don't have to worry about objections.

3. We don't have to spend time trying to convince prospects.

4. We can make our presentations short.

5. If prospects have questions, we can relax and answer as truthfully as we know how to.

Not only is this getting easier for us, we are going to leave our competition far behind!

GETTING PROSPECTS TO PAY ATTENTION.

In the previous two chapters, we talked about what goes on in our prospects' minds when they are deciding whether to do business with us or not. Now, that we know what goes on in their minds, we can begin to create a step-by-step formula for prospecting which we can not only use to our advantage but also pass on to our downlines.

But before we go into creating that formula, we need to learn how to freeze our prospects' minds. Let me make it clearer. We need to be able to bring the minds of our prospects to a complete stop and have them focus their attention on whatever we are about to say next.

Okay, you are probably thinking,

"Are you telling me that I can grab hold of someone else's mind, bring it to a complete stop, have them forget what they were thinking about, and completely focus on what I am about to say next?"

The short answer is, yes. That is what I am saying. Furthermore, doing this is very crucial because it makes absolutely no sense to talk about what we have to offer if the prospect is not focused on us and listening.

And not only are we going to get our prospects to focus on our message, we are going to make our prospects beg us for it.

Why? Because I am a full-time coward who hates rejection. So, I never give a presentation, be it for product or opportunity, unless somebody begs me for it.

How can we take an iron grip on our prospect's mind and have them focus on us, and only us?

As we have already established earlier, what we say and do when we meet a prospect is important because we will trigger certain instant reactions. These instant reactions we trigger in our prospects are due to programs that are deep-rooted in their subconscious minds.

Subconscious programs?

Yes. Here are some examples.

- If we walk into a lift and see a stranger already there, we naturally stand away from that stranger, but still facing the stranger.

- If I go to the streets, approach a stranger, and proceed to punch him in the nose, what would happen? Based on his mental programs, I would either get hit in return or he might be polite and say, "Ouch! That was rude."

- If someone smiles at you, you automatically smile back.

- If we are in a shop and a salesperson sneaks up behind us and asks, "Can I help you?" Immediately we say, "No. I am just looking."

- If someone says to us, "Hello." Without even thinking, we would return the greeting.

As we can see from the simple examples above, there are subconscious programs that will open up our prospects' minds to what we say next, and there are programs that cause a defensive response and shut down their minds to any form of communication.

So, when we are out talking to prospects, we want to be sure to use words and phrases that will help us bypass their mental defense programs, so it is easier for us to deliver our message.

If you are ready, let's move on and begin to learn some magical words and phrases to bypass our prospects' mental defense programs.

THE SURVIVAL PROGRAM.

Everybody has a survival program in their subconscious mind. This survival program exists to keep us alive and out of danger. Many of our decisions are based upon survival.

What is the problem here?

Well, the problem for us here is that the survival program makes our prospects sceptical by raising walls of distrust and disbelief in their minds. This is their subconscious survival program hard at work protecting them from being cheated of their money.

Why does the subconscious mind need to protect our money?

Because money is a very important tool to survive in today's world.

Now, let me ask you this. If our prospects do not trust and believe us, what happens?

They will make a "no" decision and not do business with us, which means we will not make any money.

Let's imagine this. What if we could use the survival program to our advantage?

Instead of triggering the survival program to put up walls of sales resistance, what if we could trigger the survival program to help us deliver our message to the decision-making part of their minds instead?

That would be wonderful, wouldn't it?

Well, it is entirely possible, and we can do so with the help of two magic words.

Most people reading this would want to know what the magic words are. And most people, if they knew these magic words, they would use them when they are talking to prospects. And if you are like most people, you can't wait to learn these words.

So, have you figured out what the two magic words are yet?

Yeah! Most people reading this would have figured out by now that the two magic words are, **"Most people."**

If this sounds weird to you, relax. Don't worry. Let's think this through together.

Why "most people" works like magic.

We humans instinctively know that one of the best ways to survive is to stay in a group. Let me give you a simple example. Say you are walking along a dark street late at night. Do you feel safer walking alone or in a group?

Of course, we feel safer in a group. This comes naturally to us because it is our survival program telling us that there is safety in numbers.

That is why the words "most people" work so well. When we say the words "most people," our prospects' subconscious minds think:

"Am I part of most people or am I part of less people? Since there is safety in numbers, I want to be part of most people and not part of less people. So, yeah, I think I am part of most people."

Just like that, with two simple words, we have turned the tables around and used the survival program to help us open doors of communication rather than put up walls of defense.

Here are some examples of using "most people" when talking to prospects.

- Most people want to travel and see the world.

- Most people want to look younger than their actual age.

- Most people are too busy for exercise.

- Most people need more money in their lives.

And that is how we take the survival program and turn it to our advantage.

Now, that wasn't too difficult, right?

THE BUSYBODY PROGRAM.

We as humans have an instinct to be curious about the world around us, and this is due to a program in our subconscious mind called, "The busybody."

We don't have time to learn everything about the busybody program, but let me give you a few key pointers so you know what we are dealing with.

Here is a real-life case study to get us started.

Case study. We are travelling along the highway. On the opposite side of the highway, there is an accident. There is a chain collision of a few cars. The firefighters, police, and ambulance service are all present at the scene of the accident and doing what they are supposed to be doing.

Now, in most cases like this, you will notice that traffic on our side of the highway will slow down.

But, why does traffic on our side of the highway slow down?

What does the accident on the opposite side have to do with traffic on this side of the highway?

Absolutely nothing! But most people are slowing down to take a better look at the accident scene on the opposite side, which does not concern them at all. That is why traffic slows down on our side of the highway where the path ahead is not affected by the accident at all.

We humans cannot help but be busybodies.

It is an instinct programmed into our subconscious mind. This is the reason why we feel this strong urge to know everything happening around us, even if it does not concern us.

This "busybody" in us becomes even more intrigued if the information is new and only a few other people on this planet have it.

Which brings us to our phrase of four magic words. Are you ready for it?

Here it is, the magic phrase: **"I just found out…"**

Now, when you say that magic phrase, it will freeze the survival program in the prospect's mind. Furthermore, it also activates the busybody program.

Why is the busybody program activated? Because when we say the words "I just found out," we are telling our prospects that we have new information. And what does the busybody program do if there is something new? It forces our prospects to lean in, focus their attention on us, and listen to this new piece of information.

Now, put yourself in the shoes of a job-hating prospect. What would go through your mind when you hear, "I just found out how we could replace our full-time income by just working from our smartphones."

What might our prospect reply?

Oftentimes, we would get the reply, "How? Tell me more!"

More examples.

- "I just found out how we can iron away our wrinkles."
- "I just found out how we don't have to work 45 years like our parents."
- "I just found out how we can take a one-week holiday every month."

And the next words from our prospects most of the time are, "How? Tell me more!"

I AM JUST CURIOUS...

One of the best ways to communicate is by asking questions. However, some questions might sound harsh or even confrontational. For example, here in Asia, the topic of money can be very sensitive. That is why when we are out there prospecting, we should never ask our prospects, "How much are you making at your current job?"

This question is often perceived as rude. A better question we could ask is, "Is an extra pay cheque what you are looking for?"

Asking a question is a good way to get a clear answer on whether or not our prospect wants the opportunity to make an extra income, without sounding rude. However, did you realise that this question seems very direct?

Which brings us to the question; what can we do about it?

How about using some magic words to soften our approach and make both the prospects and us feel more comfortable?

And the four magic words we can use are,

"I am just curious..."

Let's try it out:

"I am just curious; is an extra pay cheque what you are looking for?"

Did you notice how placing those four magic words at the beginning of our question changed the entire tone of it?

Now, our question no longer seems rude, direct, or confrontational. We can comfortably ask our question without worrying about offending our prospect.

More examples.

- I am just curious; would paying less on your next vacation make you happy?

- I am just curious; is working from your smartphone something you are looking for?

- I am just curious; what would you do if you knew the secret to getting rid of wrinkles?

As you can see, with four simple words in front of our question, we can talk to our prospects in a relaxed and comfortable manner.

Why do we want our prospects to feel relaxed and comfortable?

Because when our prospects feel comfortable, they will lean forward and listen to what we say next without raising the walls of sales resistance.

Wait, there is one problem.

If you are from Asia, you might have spotted the same problem as I did with the four magic words, "I am just curious…"

For many people in Asia, this phrase may feel very awkward and uncomfortable because that is not a very natural way for us to speak. Not only that, the problem gets worse when we try to translate it because, in some languages, the word "curious" doesn't even exist!

But don't worry. There is a very simple solution. If you look at the way people speak, in every language, there are words and phrases we are already using to soften questions that may come across as harsh or too direct.

So, instead of using the words "I am just curious," here is a five-word phrase which we can use in place of it: **"Can I ask you something?"**

Now, most English speakers will have come across this phrase before.

And if you are an English major, you might even have debated whether this phrase is acceptable in the English language. However, remember our goal here is to get our message across. Unless we can get our message into the decision-making part of our prospects' minds, we are not going to make any money.

So, let's put perfect English aside for now and focus on what is important here, which is speaking to the decision-making part of our prospects' minds.

Here are some examples.

- Can I ask you something? How would you feel if your skin got younger while you slept?
- Can I ask you something? Will you be happy if you can get discounts on your next holiday?
- Can I ask you something? How cool would it be if we could afford to go on holiday every month?

There we have it. All we need is a simple phrase of magic words in front of our question and our prospects can comfortably let us know their answer.

THE FORMULA

By Jonathan Yap

A SIMPLE FORMULA THAT WORKS.

Now that we know a little about using magic words to grab our prospects' attention, we can go back to what we discussed earlier; exactly step-by-step what goes on in our prospects' minds when we start talking about our business. We can now begin to create a formula to manage our conversation with our prospects and guide them in making a decision.

Why should we create a formula?

There are two types of people in network marketing. Those that leave their success up to chance and those that take control and responsibility for the results they create.

If we take a look at all the top distributors in network marketing, we will notice that all of them have one thing in common. They don't leave their success up to chance. They take responsibility for the results they create.

If we are serious about our network marketing business, then we need to do the same, especially when we are out there talking to prospects. We cannot use random words and hope they join. We need to have an exact formula for talking to prospects.

This will not only help us create results, but we can also pass this formula on to the people on our team so that they too can duplicate the results that we create.

Time to create our formula.

What do you think is the first step in this formula?

Well, as we talked about previously, the first question that goes through a prospect's mind is, "Who are you?"

Now, this is going to be bad news for many of us. Why? Well, think about how we have lived our lives for the last 10 years or so. Have we lived our lives to the level where we could approach our friends and family members and have them follow our lead and join us without question?

Do our friends look up to us with respect? Do the people around us look to us as a trusted source of advice?

For most people reading this, the answers to those questions would be no.

If we don't have influence over our warm market, what about the cold market?

Well, the cold hard truth is this. Most of us are not celebrities or influencers with a big list of people who are ready to join or buy anything we tell them to. But can we work on our personal brand and build a following of adoring fans?

Sure, we can. If you are already on that path, please continue. However, we need to understand that this method is a long-term strategy. We need something that will not only work now, but is also simple enough that a new distributor joining our business can learn and apply it the very day they join and begin to create results for themselves.

Now for some good news. I have discovered through my trials and errors that we can bypass this first question and move on directly to the second question in the prospect's mind, "Can I trust you?"

If we know how to build trust and rapport with our prospects, they will naturally want to do business with us. After all, nobody likes to do business with people they don't trust.

So, let us move on and focus on the most important question in our prospects' minds: **Can I trust you?**

STEP #1:
BUILDING INSTANT
RAPPORT.

As we have already learnt earlier in this book, we can have the best products and compensation plan on earth, but if our prospects do not trust and believe us, then they are not going to want to do business with us.

When it comes to building rapport and trust with prospects, let me give you some things that are **NOT** necessary:

1. Being honest.

2. Having integrity.

3. Being sincere.

4. Having the prospect's best interest at heart.

Many of you might be scratching your head right now and thinking, "Wait! Aren't those important if we want to build trust with our prospects? Are you saying to be dishonest?"

Let me explain. I am not saying to be dishonest. Honesty, integrity, and sincerity are all good qualities. We should practice them because it makes us good people.

What I am saying is that the human mind looks for specific things to create trust and these qualities are not part of those things. So, when it comes to building trust and rapport, these qualities are not necessary. If you don't believe it, let's do some case studies.

Case Study #1. Have you ever done a presentation where you were honest with your prospect, conducted yourself with high integrity, and had the prospect's best interest at heart, but they didn't believe you and told you no?

Yes. We have all been through it.

Case study #2. Let's talk about con men. Their profession is all about getting people to trust them so that they can cheat people out of their money.

Are con men honest? Does cheating people display high integrity? Do they have their victim's best interests at heart?

No! Of course not!

However, these con men have the ability to get honest hardworking people to give them their hard-earned money. Obviously, these con men are using specific skills to gain people's trust, within seconds of meeting them, and getting their message inside of their victims' heads.

Can we learn these rapport-building skills too? Yes, of course we can!

Let's start with a smile.

Well, for starters, we could smile. Now, some of you might be thinking, "Smile? Why smile?"

Let me briefly explain something about the human mind which will help us understand why smiling is important in rapport-building.

All of us have an important survival program inside our subconscious minds that warns us of danger and keeps us alive. Sales resistance is simply part of our survival program.

How does this work in real life? Let's say we are sitting on a bench in the park and a little child runs up to us and stops in front of us, about a metre away. The child looks at us cautiously. It is obvious to us the child is trying to determine if we are a threat or not.

So, what do we do out of instinct? We smile! When we smile, we are telling the other person that we are not a threat and it is safe to interact with us.

And what happens most of the time when we smile at someone? Well, most of the time, the other person smiles back because we have been socially conditioned to do so. There is a program inside our minds that says, "If someone smiles at you, smile back."

It is a really stupid program, but it is there.

Now, I am not saying that a smile alone will always create trust, belief, and rapport. What I am saying is that a smile is a great way to begin a conversation because when we smile, our chances go way up, and when we frown, our chances go way down.

So, practice smiling because it works.

Same-Same.

In Asia, there is a popular saying: "We like people who are same-same."

What this simply means is that people tend to like and trust other people who are the same as them. So, when they talk to people who don't think the same way as them, they tend to put up walls of disbelief. This is because, inside our subconscious minds, we have a program that says:

"I can trust people who are the same as me and think the same way."

This is why we like people who drink the same brand of beer, support the same sports teams, have the same hobbies, and so on.

Imagine this. I am from Singapore. Let's say I take a trip to Germany and while I am there, I meet another person from Singapore. Immediately I feel closer to that Singaporean than all the Germans around me. There is an instant connection and bond because that Singaporean is "same-same" with me.

Now, imagine you were in that same situation. You were in a foreign land and you met someone from your country. Wouldn't you feel an instant connection with that person?

Yes, of course.

Now, I did not know this when I first started in network marketing and looking back, one of the biggest mistakes I made was that when I talked to prospects, I would point out our differences. I would say things like, "Your job is stupid. My business opportunity is smart. Join me."

From first-hand experience, I can tell you that pointing out your differences is not a very good idea when talking to prospects.

How about you? Have you ever made this mistake before?

So, to build instant rapport, what we should be doing when talking to prospects is to instead tell them things that they already believe.

When you tell your prospects something they already believe, their subconscious mind says,

"Wow! You think the same way as me. That means you are a genius, like me! I can start to believe the things you say."

Could you think of some things that our prospects would already believe?

Here are some examples.

For health and nutrition:

- Nobody enjoys being sick.
- People want to live longer.
- Being fit is better than being ill.
- When our children fall sick, our hearts break.
- Growing old can be painful.

For skincare:

- We all hate wrinkles.
- Nobody likes acne.
- It is normal to want to slow down the ageing process.
- We all want more beautiful and radiant skin.

- People love to look younger than their age.

For diet products:

- Losing weight can be really hard.
- It is difficult to find time to exercise.
- People hate diets.
- Starving ourselves will kill us.
- Life is not worth living if we can't eat our favourite foods.

For travel:

- Travelling can be expensive.
- Everyone has a dream vacation they are longing for.
- Everybody loves discounts when they travel.
- We all deserve at least one vacation a year.
- Family holidays create the best memories.

For business opportunities:

- Life is getting expensive.
- Prices for everything are going up.
- Salaries are stagnant.
- It is hard to get a raise nowadays.
- Most people would love to fire their boss.
- We don't have to be stuck as an employee forever.
- Being our own boss would give us more freedom.
- Choosing our own working hours would be awesome.
- Having extra income every month would help tremendously.

- Working two days in a week is better than working five days in a week.
- Getting paid a full-time income for working 2 weeks in a month is a dream come true.
- We all need to work less and travel more.

Did you notice how easy it was to agree with most of these statements?

Now, that is the exact feeling we want our prospects to feel when we are talking to them. There is no point in talking about our business or products until the prospect is in total rapport with us.

Remember, one of the things that sets the professionals apart from the amateurs is that professionals know to only present their business to people who trust and believe them.

So, let's keep this in mind and practice it, because we are network marketing professionals.

LET'S GET EVEN BETTER AT BUILDING RAPPORT.

We now know that by telling our prospects a single fact they already believe, we are telling our prospects that we have the same beliefs and see the world from the same viewpoint. In doing so, we build that bond and feeling of trust with our prospects.

So, the question I have for you now is this. What could be better than telling our prospects a fact that they already believe to be true?

Well, how about telling our prospects two facts that they already believe?

Yes. When we tell our prospects two facts that they already believe to be true, we take our rapport-building to the next level. After two facts, our prospects start to feel really comfortable with us and now, more than before, instead of leaning back and not wanting to listen to the good things we have to say, they lean in and want to listen and trust what we say next.

And that is what we want, isn't it?

We want to take the ideas from inside of our heads and have them transferred into our prospects' heads so they can decide if what we have to offer serves them or not.

So, here are some examples.

For health and nutrition:

- It is normal to want to live longer, and nobody enjoys being sick.

- Falling sick is no joke. Especially when our children fall sick, our hearts break.

- We all love to age slower because growing old can be painful.

For skincare:

- Wrinkles are ugly and that is why we all want to slow down the ageing process.

- We all want more beautiful skin. That is why nobody likes acne.

- Everybody hates growing old and that is why most people love to look younger than their age.

For diet products:

- People hate diets because starving ourselves will kill us.

- It is difficult to find time for exercise, therefore losing weight can be really hard.

- We all have favourite foods. That is why most diet programs are difficult to follow.

For travel:

- Travelling can be expensive. That is why most people wait for discounts to book their travels.

- Everyone has a dream vacation they are longing for. The problem is that travelling can be really expensive.

- We all deserve at least one vacation a year. After all, family holidays create the best memories.

For business opportunities:

- Life is getting expensive and the prices for everything are going up.

- The cost of living is going up, and that is why having extra income every month would help tremendously.

- Our salaries are stagnant because it is hard to get a raise nowadays.

- Most people would love to fire their boss instead of being stuck as an employee forever.

- Working two days in a week is better than working five days in a week. After all, we all need to work less and travel more.

What about magic words?

By simply telling our prospects two facts that we can all agree on, magic happens. We gain instant rapport. However, we want to be sure that we deliver our rapport-building message to the decision-making part of their minds. For that, we can use the sequence of two magic words, **"Most people..."**

Some examples of using "most people" when talking to prospects:

For travel:

- Most people want to travel and see the world. In fact, most people have a dream vacation they are longing for.

- Most people know that travelling can be expensive. That is why most people look for discounts when they book their travels.

- Most families love creating beautiful memories while on vacation. After all, family holidays create the best memories.

- Most people deserve at least one holiday a year. And what most people do is look for the best deals when booking their plane tickets.

For skincare:

- Most people hate acne and most people want more beautiful skin.

- Most people would love to get rid of wrinkles and look younger than their actual age.

- Most people would love to reverse the ageing process and have younger, more radiant skin.

For diet products:

- Most people hate starving themselves. That is why most diet programmes don't work.

- Most people are too busy for exercise. That is why most people find losing weight hard.

- Most people want to lose weight fast. The problem is that most people love eating their favourite foods too much to give them up.

For business opportunities:

- Most people need more money in their lives because most jobs don't pay enough.

- Most people hate their jobs. And most people would love to fire their boss if they could.

- Most people agree that working two days a week is better than working five days a week. After all, we all need to work less and travel more.

- Most people say that the cost of living is going up. That is why most people agree that having extra income every month would help tremendously.

Let's review.

Okay. Let's put everything we have talked about on building instant rapport together and come up with a step-by-step process.

1. Smile.

2. Use a magic word sequence then tell our prospect a fact that we can all believe.

3. Use a magic word sequence again then tell our prospect another fact we can all agree to be true.

Now, let's see how this looks.

- \<Smile\>
  "Most people hate dieting.
  And most people know that starving our bodies is crazy."

- \<Smile\>
  "Most people agree that the tropical sun here really damages our skin.
  And most people want their skin to be soft and radiant, not damaged."

- <Smile>

  "Most people agree that having a job can be stressful and not fun,

  but we still go to work because most people need to make a living."

- <Smile>

  "Most people would agree that bills eat up most of our monthly salary.

  That is why most people know that having an extra income would be useful."

- <Smile>

  "Most people want to give their children the best in life.

  However, most people know that the problem is that everything is so expensive nowadays."

- <Smile>

  "Most people would love to travel more.

  The only thing is, as most people would agree, travelling can be really expensive."

Now, that wasn't too difficult, right?

So, there we have it. Building rapport with our prospects is not difficult and only takes a few seconds. Using our instant rapport-building techniques in this book, we don't need to spend hours on mindless social chit-chat and relationship-building.

Especially in today's world where people have very short attention spans. All the more, people are going to make instant decisions. But that is not an issue for us.

We are network marketing professionals, not amateurs. We know how to manage the first few seconds when we talk to a prospect by using our instant rapport-building techniques and getting them to make an immediate decision to lean in, listen, and believe the good things we say about our products or opportunity.

Now, let us move on to the next step in our formula.

STEP #2: ICEBREAKERS.

Now, for those that are not familiar with this term, you are probably thinking, "What are icebreakers?"

I'll give you the short answer. Icebreakers are simply words or phrases we say to introduce a new topic into a conversation.

We can use icebreakers to change our conversation from social chit-chat to introducing our products or opportunity to our prospects.

Our icebreakers do not have to be very long. Most times they are only a sentence or two. At the end of the icebreaker, our prospect is going to decide if we are interesting to them or not.

If our prospect decides that we are not interesting, then they will refuse to engage in our conversation any further. This is how the human mind works. The human mind is designed to eliminate conversations that are not interesting.

How do we know what to say when introducing our product or business?

Well, we listen to the prospect, of course.

Imagine we were talking to a prospect and in our conversation, that prospect told us that he hates his job but he has no choice but to keep it because he needs the money for his family. So, what might we say to this prospect?

Remember earlier we talked about building rapport?

After we use some of our rapport-building techniques, we can move on and use an icebreaker to introduce our solution; in the case of our job-hating prospect, introducing our business opportunity would make sense.

Here are some examples.

- You can fire your boss and be your own boss.

- We don't have to work for 45 years like our parents.

- You can work from home and still make a full-time income.

What do professional network marketers do when using icebreakers?

Now, we could simply insert an icebreaker statement or two after building rapport, but we are not going to do that. Why? Because we are not amateurs; we are professionals!

So, what we need to do first is take an iron grip of our prospects' minds and have them focus on us, and only us. And we can do so by triggering the "busybody" program in their minds.

There is a four-word sequence which enables us to do so. The magic phrase is, **"I just found out…"**

Here are some examples.

For health and nutrition.

- I just found out how we can wake up every morning feeling like a million dollars.

- I just found out how we can fall asleep within minutes of our heads touching our pillows.

- I just found out how to have energy all day long without taking caffeine.

For skincare.

- I just found out how we can iron away our wrinkles.
- I just found out how we can make our skin younger while we sleep.
- I just found out how to get rid of acne once and for all.

For travel.

- I just found out how we can take a one-week holiday every month.
- I just found out how to get the best discounts ever.
- I just found out how to travel like a king at a discounted rate.

For diet programs.

- I just found out how to lose weight without starving ourselves.
- I just found out how to eat ice cream and still lose weight.
- I just found out how to keep a slim belly without crazy starvation diets.

For business opportunities.

- I just found out how we can fire our boss and be our own boss.
- I just found out how we can stay home with our children and still earn a full-time income.
- I just found out how we don't have to work for 45 years like our parents.

- I just found out how we can make an extra pay cheque every month.

- I just found out how we can get a raise without our boss knowing about it.

And most of the time, the next words from our prospects are, "How? Tell me more!"

Can you come up with some icebreakers of your own? Sure you can. It would be very beneficial to you if you took some time to write down some icebreakers of your very own which you can use for your specific product or opportunity.

And when you are done, we can move on to the next step in our formula, which is **collecting decisions.**

STEP #3:
COLLECTING DECISIONS.

Is collecting decisions the same as closing?

Yes, that is exactly what it is. Well, to be more exact, there are two parts to closing. Collecting the mental "yes" decision from the prospect is the first of the two parts in closing. We will talk about the second part later in this book. For now, let's focus on collecting decisions.

But wait, don't we have to do a presentation first?

The answer is no. What we are going to do is close the prospect first, then we do a presentation to support their decision. In fact, you and I should never again do a presentation unless our prospect has made a mental decision to be our customer or join our business.

For those of you who are confused at this point, think back to our chapter on case studies. We have already established that the human mind makes decisions almost instantly, **BEFORE** all the facts, figures, and information.

Isn't that what our presentation is all about?

Isn't our presentation a showcase of information about our products and opportunity?

This means that our prospects are going to decide either "yes" or "no" before our presentation even begins. So, we are going to collect our prospects' decisions first.

If a prospect makes a "no" decision, then there is no need for a presentation. Forcing prospects who have made a "no" decision to sit through a presentation is a bad idea. The prospect will be irritated, leaning back with folded arms, impatiently waiting for us to finish so that he or she can reject us.

Ouch! We not only waste everybody's time, we set ourselves up for unnecessary rejection.

Now, if a prospect makes a "yes" decision, then we move on and do a presentation to support that "yes" decision.

How do we collect decisions?

Well, we ask the prospect, of course. When we leave the decision entirely up to our prospects, we take the pressure off everyone.

Here is an example of a question we could ask our prospects to see what their decision is. To a prospect who wants to make more money, we could say:

"Is an extra pay cheque what you are looking for?"

Now, our prospect can make a decision and let us know if having an extra pay cheque is something that he or she is looking for.

So, asking a question is a good way to get a clear answer on whether or not a prospect wants what we have to offer. However, did you realise that our decision-collecting question seems very direct, kind of harsh, or even rude?

We definitely don't want to come across as rude and offend our prospects. Which brings us to this question:

What can we do about it?

How about using the magic words we talked about earlier to soften our approach and make both the prospects and us feel more comfortable?

Here are the two sequences of magic words:

- I am just curious...
- Can I ask you something?

Here are some examples.

For skincare.

- I am just curious, how would you feel if your skin got younger while you slept?
- Can I ask you something? What would you do if you knew the secret to getting rid of wrinkles?
- I am just curious, is getting rid of acne once and for all something you would like to know more about?

For travel.

- I am just curious, would paying less on your next vacation make you happy?
- I am just curious, wouldn't it be amazing if we could afford to take our kids on a vacation every month?
- Can I ask you something? Is it okay with you if you could take a one-week holiday every month?

For health and nutrition.

- I am just curious, wouldn't it be awesome if you could wake up every morning feeling like a million dollars?

- I am just curious, would falling asleep within minutes of your head touching your pillow work for you?

- Can I ask you something? Is having energy all day long without taking caffeine something that you would love to know more about?

For diet programs.

- I am just curious, does losing weight without starving ourselves make sense to you?

- I am just curious, does losing weight while eating our favourite foods sound good to you?

- Can I ask you something? Would knowing the secret to a slim belly without crazy starvation diets make you happy?

For business opportunities.

- Can I ask you something? Is working from your smartphone something you are looking for?

- I am just curious, would never showing up for work again work for you?

- I am just curious, what would you say to an extra pay cheque every month?

Can you think of some closing questions for your business?

Take some time and write down some closing questions which are specific to your products and opportunity. And when you are done with that, we can move on to the next step in our formula: **presentations.**

STEP #4: PRESENTATION.
(PART 1)

The next step in our formula is the presentation, which should be the easiest part of our formula. Our prospects have already made a "yes" decision, and they are leaning in to listen and pick up some information to support their decision. No convincing or manipulation needed.

And what better way to start our chapter on this than with an interesting question?

"When we are introducing our business or product to a prospect for the very first time, should we do a long presentation or a short presentation?"

I remember when I first started in network marketing, I did long presentations which lasted between two to three hours. After 46 months and countless rejections, I started to wonder if people enjoyed three-hour-long presentations where I talked about the network marketing company, the company founder, products, and compensation plan.

So, there was only one thing for me to do. I had to run an experiment to find out. And here is what I did. Whenever I talked to a prospect, I would ask my prospect this question before I proceeded to a presentation:

"I have a three-hour version and a five-minute version. Which would you prefer?"

The result.

I asked this question to about 60 different people, and what intrigued me was that every one of them made the same choice: the five-minute version. The result was very clear to me.

Most people, when you first introduce your business or product to them, want a short presentation, not a long presentation.

Why is this so? Well, the way I see it is that everybody has a very limited amount of time. Therefore, people don't have time for all our ideas and agendas. There are plenty of other things in their lives which require their time.

Can we really do a presentation in five minutes?

In the beginning, this was a problem for me. I was never taught how to do a five-minute presentation. I had never done a presentation that lasted less than two hours before. But after many rounds of trial and error, I managed to come up with a short presentation which was only five minutes long.

For a while, I was very proud that I could do a presentation which lasted only five minutes long. Not to mention, my sign-up rates went way up.

And then I met Tom Schreiter and here is what I learnt from him.

What is better than a five-minute presentation?

A one-minute presentation, of course!

Tom made me realise that five minutes was a really long time for a presentation. The reality is that when I first introduce my business to someone, I only need one minute to do an entire presentation.

Now, just to be clear, I am not talking about some kind of teaser to get prospects interested in our products or business. That should have already happened in the icebreaker step.

When I say a one-minute presentation, I am talking about a complete presentation with all the facts, figures, and information that our prospects need to comfortably move forward in the decision-making process.

Sound impossible?

If you think that it is impossible to give an entire presentation in just one minute, you are not alone. That was exactly what I thought too!

However, if we take some time to think about it, everything we have learnt in life seemed difficult and impossible before we learnt how.

So, relax. Just like we learnt how to read and write, we can learn how to give an entire presentation in one minute, or even less.

So, if you are ready, let's get started.

A simple solution.

There are a few different solutions to reducing our presentation down to one minute. The two solutions are:

1. We can talk really fast.

2. We take information out of our presentation.

I think we can all agree that talking very fast might not be a good solution. I don't see a way to talk fast enough to get our entire two-hour presentation done in one minute.

So, that leaves us with the other solution. We would have to take out information which is not useful at this stage.

Our standard opportunity presentations.

Let's take a look at the presentations we usually give at opportunity meetings. What do we normally talk about?

- The year the company was founded.
- The company mission statement.
- Financial strength of the company.
- Sales turnover of the previous year.
- Awards the company has won.
- The company founder and his achievements.
- The wealth and riches of the company founder.
- All the charities the company founder donates to.
- The patent numbers on our products.
- Explanation on the secret ingredient in our products.
- The science behind our products.
- Pictures of our scientists.
- Biased testimonials from people who love our products.
- A detailed look into the compensation plan.
- Draw circles stacked in the shape of a pyramid.
- Show pictures of pay cheques.

- Talk about our god-like upline leader.

- Show pictures of our upline leader's car.

- Watch videos of our upline leader walking on water.

- And, much more!

Okay, I got a little carried away at the end there. But you get the point.

Just take a look at the list. That is a long list of things to be talking about.

And the worst part is that this list is nowhere near completion. There is more!

Can we see now why our presentations are taking so long?

Let me ask you this. Is talking about all those things we listed necessary?

What if our prospects are not going to join?

Do our prospects need to know all those facts, figures, and information, if they are not joining?

Of course, the answer is no. If they are not going to join, then all the information that we include in our presentation is useless to them.

But what if our prospects want to join?

Well, if our prospect wants to join, then they can learn those facts, figures, and information later on in training.

Now we can relax and begin the process of removing things from our presentation.

What can we remove from our presentation?

We can start with the company and company founder.

We can remove the vision and mission statement, sales turnover, the awards which the company has won, the pictures of the golden toilet seat in the executive bathroom, the boring company video that puts prospects to sleep, the history of the company founder, pictures of the company founder's car, and pictures of every person in the management team.

If our prospects join us in the business, then they can learn about all these things in training. And, some of them who join might even pay a visit to the company's main office to try out that golden toilet seat for themselves.

But at this stage, all this information is not necessary to our prospects. So, let's save everyone time by removing them from our presentation.

Next, let's look at our products.

What about our products?

Are there facts and information which are not useful that we can remove?

Let's take out the patent numbers, the 300 biased testimonials, the 200-page research report, pictures of the scientists in lab coats, pictures of the factory, and we can stop reading the product label like our prospects do not know how to read.

While we are at it, let's take out the explanation on how our secret ingredient can only be found in a secret cave in Atlantis, and the pictures and videos of the mermaids our company has to specially hire to harvest the secret ingredient.

Going back to what we said earlier, if our prospect is not going to join, then all this information is not necessary. And if our prospect joins, we can talk about it in training.

Looks like we are making progress in getting our presentation down to one minute.

The compensation plan.

Do we really need to describe each and every bonus?

Do we have to explain what is qualifying volume and business volume?

Do we need to go through each rank in detail?

I bet you already know the answer to all the questions above. The answer to all the questions is "no." Once our prospects join us in our business, then all this information is necessary. And, they can learn about all these in training.

So, what information should we include?

Now, you are probably thinking, "If I take all this information out of my presentation, then there is nothing for me to talk about. So, what do I talk about?!"

Well, remember, prospects don't have time for our agenda. They only have time to focus on their own agenda. So, doesn't it make sense to make our presentation focused on what our prospects want to know?

Now, we could jump immediately into a presentation, but we are not going to do that.

Remember, we are not mere amateurs. We are professional network marketers. So before we move into the presentation, we want to ensure that our prospects have disabled their mental defense programs and are leaning forward and eager to listen to the information we are about to share.

How do we do that?

Well, remember earlier on when we talked about humans being creatures of reaction?

And, do you recall when we talked about using magic word sequences that would cause our prospects to react by disabling their mental defense programs?

So, it is obvious. We can get our prospects leaning forward and eagerly waiting for our presentation, by using some magic word sequences.

Are you ready for it? Here are the two magic sentences:

"I can tell you everything you need to know in one minute. Do you have one minute now?"

There we have it. Two simple sentences that work like magic and will have our prospects looking forward to a presentation.

Let's see how this would work in a real-world situation.

Imagine you and I are co-workers. It is a slow day at work, so we decide to take a little two-hour coffee break. So there we are, chatting about life, and we start to talk about our dead-end jobs.

Then I say, "Looks like we are not getting a pay increase this year. Ever feel like we are overworked and underpaid?"

You reply, "Yeah! Not only that, our boss doesn't do anything, and he gets paid more than us!"

I nod my head and say, "You know it! Wouldn't it be cool if we made more money than our boss?"

You agree, saying, "Yeah!"

Then I say, "I would be able to take my family on an extra holiday every year with that kind of money. What would you do with all that extra money?"

You reply, "Family holidays sound great. After all, the memories we create will stay in our children's hearts forever."

I reply by saying, "I hear you! Say, you know what, I just found out not too long ago how you and I can make some extra cash every month without our boss knowing about it. What do you think of that?"

You cautiously reply, "The extra money would be useful. What is this all about?"

I quickly reply, "Well, I can tell you everything you need to know in one minute. Do you have one minute now?"

What might you say to that?

Almost everyone would say, "Yes."

But why do these two sentences work like magic?

Let's put ourselves in the position of our prospects and think about it for a moment. What might be going through their minds when they hear our two magic sentences?

- "It is only one minute, so we are going to get this over with quickly."
- "I don't think one minute is enough time for a sales pitch. It is barely enough time for a few pieces of information."
- "Even if it is a sales pitch, I think I can keep my resistance up for one minute."
- "Only one minute? Might as well listen just in case this information is important."
- "It is only one minute. Not some boring three-hour presentation."

Just imagine, by simply using two sentences, we take away the stress and pressure, remove the scepticism and salesman alarms from our prospects' minds, and we get a favourable reaction from our prospects that is to our advantage.

Now, our prospects will lean forward, eagerly anticipating our presentation.

STEP #4: PRESENTATION.
(PART 2)

What do our prospects want to know?

At this point in the prospecting process, our prospects would have already made the mental "yes" decision to do business with us. So, what they are looking for at this stage is some basic information to support their "yes" decision, so that they can comfortably move forward and join our business or be our customer.

So, once we give them the basic information they are looking for, our prospects can comfortably move forward with one of three choices.

Choice #1: I want to do business with you.

Choice #2: I don't want to do business with you.

Choice #3: Everything sounds good, but I have a question.

So, what basic information are prospects looking for?

All we have to do at this point of the prospecting process is answer four simple questions. That is all our prospects need. Here are the four questions we must answer:

1. "What kind of business is this?"

2. "How much money can I make?"

3. "Exactly what do I have to do to earn this money?"

4. "Can I do it?"

And that is it! Simple. Are we starting to see that doing a presentation in one minute is actually possible?

"What kind of business is this?"

Earlier in this book, we established that we are in the decision-making business. But we are not going to tell the prospect that this business is about decision-making.

Why? Because what our prospects want to know is what business our network marketing company is in.

So, let's give our prospects what they want and let them know if our company is dealing with skincare, nutrition, weight loss, travel, etc.

However, the problem is that those terms are very vague and don't give our prospects a clear picture of what we do. We need to give our prospects a very clear idea of what it is that we do. If not, they will be confused, and a confused mind will always make a "no" decision.

How can we give our prospects a clear picture of what it is that we do?

Two words: **"Which means."**

When we are describing our business, all we need to do is to use the words "which means" and then follow up by stating a problem that our products solve.

Let me give you some examples.

- "We are in the travel business, which means we show people how to get big discounts on their vacations."

- "We are in the skincare business, which means that we have a serum that makes your skin look younger while you sleep."

- "We are in the wellness business, which means we have a delicious juice that helps people feel like a million dollars and have more energy during the day."

- "We are in the stress management business, which means we have special oils that help people calm their minds at night so that they have better sleep quality."

Simple, right?

Just by using two magic words, our prospects now know exactly what kind of business we are in.

Now, there are a few things you would want to take note of when describing your business.

1. Don't make it too long. If you do, it sounds like a sales pitch. So, stick to using just one or two sentences to explain the problem your product solves.

2. Stay away from network marketing jargon. I'm talking about words like scientific breakthrough, patented technology, proprietary, etc.

These types of words set off the "salesman alarm" in our prospects' minds, and that is not what we want. We want to answer their internal questions **WITHOUT** setting off the "salesman alarm," because once it is set off, it is game over.

"How much money can I make?"

Well, if I was looking at a business opportunity, I would certainly ask this question, wouldn't you?

But we don't have to worry. This question is easy to answer. What we do is simply choose an amount that matches what our prospect is looking for.

How do we know how much our prospects want? Simple. Here are two ways.

The first way is to use a little common sense. If our prospect is looking for some extra money every month to help pay off some bills, then we can talk about making an extra few hundred dollars every month. If our prospect wants to quit and never work in a job again, then we need to talk about making a full-time income.

So, we want to match the amount we talk about to what our prospects want. It would not make sense to talk about making a few hundred dollars extra every month if our prospect is looking to replace a full-time income.

The second way is to simply ask the prospect. We could say:

"Just curious, how much extra money are you looking to make every month?"

There we have it. Two simple ways to know how much money we should be talking about when we talk to our prospects. Just take note, each situation is different so just choose the way that works best for each particular situation.

Now, let's move on to the third question.

"Exactly what do I have to do to earn this money?"

Many network marketers don't answer this question when they do presentations, and that is a huge mistake.

Why? Because this is the most important question we need to answer.

Let's be professional and do what professional network marketers do, which is answer their question, "Exactly what do I have to do to earn this money?"

To be fair, if we were looking for a business opportunity, wouldn't this question be on our minds as well?

Now, you must be thinking, "If we don't describe the compensation plan, explain each bonus and percentage, go through the different rank levels, and so on, then what do we talk about?"

First, let's take a look at some bad examples of how to answer this question.

- This business is not about sales. It is about sharing.
- Just talk to your friends.
- Our product sells itself, so you just need to use it.

Ouch! Did those answers sound silly? Did you cringe?

What we have to do is give our prospects a general idea of the activities they would have to do to earn the money we talked about.

Here is an example of explaining the activities to our prospects. See what you think of it.

- All you have to do is, between you, and everybody you talk to, and everybody they talk to forever and ever and ever, is find four or five people who feel the same way you do. People who love to sleep better at night and who would like to earn a full-time income helping others do the same.

Now, that sounds a lot better than the previous three examples. However, it still seems a little bit confusing, don't you think?

- All you have to do is start using the product so you can sleep better at night. Then, find about five people who feel the same way you do. People who want to sleep better at night and who would like to earn a full-time income helping others do the same. Now, you can take a month to find these five people, or a year, or even ten years. How fast or slow is entirely up to you.

Okay! Doesn't that sound a lot clearer?

Our prospects now know exactly what they have to do to earn that extra money every month. Plus, we take the pressure of finding five people off by letting our prospects know that how fast or slow they want to build this business is up to them.

We can move on to the next question.

"Can I do it?"

The thought of finding five people might feel uncomfortable to many people. And we can't blame them. After all, they have never learnt about prospecting or about "finding five people" for their business in school.

But we have training and coaching sessions for that, don't we?

So, let's be nice to our prospects and let them know that we have training and coaching sessions available, so they don't have to worry.

We could say this.

- Now, there may be a problem. Most people, when they first get started in our business, don't know how to find these five people or what to say to them. That is why we have an education system that shows us exactly how to do this business, step-by-step. So, just like we learnt how to walk, talk, and read a book, we can learn how to do this business.

Wasn't that easy? Just a few simple sentences and now our prospect knows that we have help and support available for them.

Are you ready to put it all together?

If you are ready to take what we have learnt about presentations and put it all together, then let's move on to the next chapter.

STEP #4: PRESENTATION.
(PART 3)

Putting together a complete presentation.

We sure have talked a lot about presentations in this book. Are you ready to put together a complete one-minute presentation from start to finish?

Let's begin with this scenario.

Imagine that we are taking an extended coffee break at work. There we are, sitting in the pantry, sipping our coffee and chatting away.

You turn the conversation from a social chat to a business conversation tactfully using your rapport-building techniques, icebreakers, and closing questions.

One of our colleagues says to you, "What is it all about? Please tell me more."

You say, "I can give you a complete presentation, but it would take an entire minute. Do you have one minute now?"

Our colleague replies, "Yes, now would be great." What might your reply be?

For skincare:

"If you want to earn an extra $500 a month, you need to do these three things.

Number one: Don't change. Continue to recommend and promote things you like, such as your favourite restaurant or movie.

Number two: We are in the skincare business, which means we help people get younger skin every night while they sleep.

Number three: All you have to do is start using our product and reverse the ageing process. Then, sometime in your lifetime, find about five people who feel the same way you do. People who also have a passion for looking younger and who would like to earn money helping others do the same.

Show these people how they can have a part-time business helping others have better skin. And then you would earn an extra $500 a month.

Now, you don't have to find all four or five people right away. Pace yourself. You can take a month, a year, or even ten years. How fast or slow is entirely up to you.

Now, there may be a problem. Most people, when they first get started in our business, don't know how to find these five people or what to say to them. That is why we have an education system that shows us exactly how to do this business, step-by-step.

So, just like we learnt how to walk, talk, and read a book, we can learn how to do this business."

For nutrition:

"If you want to earn an extra $1000 a month, you need to do these three things.

Number one: Don't change. Continue to recommend and promote things you like, such as your favourite restaurant or movie.

Number two: We are in the nutrition business, which means we help people sleep better and wake up feeling like a million dollars.

Number three: All you have to do is start using our product and start sleeping better every night. Then, sometime in your lifetime, find about five people who feel the same way you do. People who also have a passion for better sleep and long-lasting energy throughout the day, and who would like to earn money helping others do the same.

Show these people how they can have a part-time business helping others have better sleep and more energy. And then you would earn an extra $1000 a month.

Now, you don't have to find all four or five people right away. Pace yourself. You can take a month, a year, or even ten years. How fast or slow is entirely up to you.

Now, there may be a problem. Most people, when they first get started in our business, don't know how to find these five people or what to say to them. That is why we have an education system that shows us exactly how to do this business, step-by-step.

So, just like we learnt how to walk, talk, and read a book, we can learn how to do this business."

For diet programs:

"If you want to earn $5000 a month, you need to do these three things.

Number one: Don't change. Continue to recommend and promote things you like, such as your favourite restaurant or movie.

Number two: We are in the weight-loss business, which means we help people lose weight without resorting to starvation diets.

Number three: All you have to do is start using our product and experience the benefits. Then, sometime in your lifetime, find about five people who feel the same way you do. People who also have a passion for looking good and feeling great, and who would like to earn money helping others do the same.

Show these people how they can have a part-time business helping others slim down without starving themselves. And then you would earn an extra $5000 a month.

Now, you don't have to find all four or five people right away. Pace yourself. You can take a month, a year, or even ten years. How fast or slow is entirely up to you.

Now, there may be a problem. Most people, when they first get started in our business, don't know how to find these five people or what to say to them. That is why we have an education system that shows us exactly how to do this business, step-by-step.

So, just like we learnt how to walk, talk, and read a book, we can learn how to do this business."

For travel:

"If you want to earn an extra $5000 a month, you need to do these three things.

Number one: Don't change. Continue to recommend and promote things you like, such as your favourite restaurant or movie.

Number two: We are in the travel business, which means we help people get the best discounts for their travels.

Number three: All you have to do is start paying less for travelling. Then, sometime in your lifetime, find about five people who feel the same way you do. People who also have a passion for paying less when they travel, and who would like to earn money helping others do the same.

Show these people how they can have a part-time business helping others get the best deals for their travels. And then you would earn an extra $5000 a month.

Now, you don't have to find all four or five people right away. Pace yourself. You can take a month, a year, or even ten years. How fast or slow is entirely up to you.

Now, there may be a problem. Most people, when they first get started in our business, don't know how to find these five people or what to say to them. That is why we have an education system that shows us exactly how to do this business, step-by-step.

So, just like we learnt how to walk, talk, and read a book, we can learn how to do this business."

Done.

That wasn't too difficult, was it? Did you also notice from the examples that we can use our one-minute presentation for different products and different income goals?

The best part is that there is no pressure on anyone. Now, our prospects can comfortably make one of three decisions:

Choice #1: I want to do business with you.

Choice #2: I don't want to do business with you.

Choice #3: I have a question or two.

We will go deeper into the choices our prospects make in the next chapter when we talk about the last step in our formula: **the call to action.**

STEP #5: CALL TO ACTION.

Remember earlier in this book we talked about how there are two parts to closing?

The first part of closing happened in Step #3, where our prospects made a mental decision whether to do business with us or not.

Then in our presentation, which is Step #4, we gave our prospects information to support their mental decisions by answering their four internal questions.

Now, in Step #5, the call to action, which is the second part of closing, we simply let our prospects know that it is time to act upon their decision.

Before we move forward.

Before we indicate to our prospects that it is time to act upon their decision, it is only polite and professional that we let our prospects know that our presentation has come to an end and we should check if they have any questions.

First, let's talk about letting our prospects know that the presentation has ended with two simple sentences.

Sentence #1: "And that is it!"

Just imagine if we did not let our prospects know that our presentation has come to an end. There would be an awkward silence as they look at us, waiting for us to continue the presentation while we stare at them, waiting for them to tell us their decision.

So, let's be professional and cut out this awkward silence by simply letting our prospects know that our presentation has ended by saying, "And that is it."

Sentence #2: "The rest is up to you."

With this sentence, we let our prospects know that we are not going to pressure them into buying anything or joining our business. We have delivered our information and now our prospects can choose what they would like to do next.

No pressure on anyone. And, there is no rejection either. Why?

Because we let our prospects choose yes, choose no, or ask a question.

We are all comfortable with any one of those choices. What would make everyone uncomfortable is if we try to high-pressure and force our prospects into a "yes" decision. So, let's keep things polite and comfortable for everyone and let our prospects make up their minds on their own.

Next, we should check if our prospects have any questions.

It is only professional to check if our prospects have any questions. And here is a question I love to use at the end of my one-minute presentations:

"What would you like to know next?"

There will be prospects who have a question or two. That is why I recommend asking this at the end of our presentation to check if the prospect has any questions.

Now, if our prospects have any questions, all we need to do is to answer their questions as honestly as we can. That is all.

Remember, we are not here to manipulate them into joining us in our business. What we are here to do is make sure they have all the information they need to validate their decision. Then they can comfortably let us know if their decision is a yes or no.

The call to action.

Now that our presentation is over, and our prospects have no further questions, it is time for them to take action. We want to encourage our prospects to take action, but at the same time, we don't want to come off as pushy. That is not too difficult and here is how we are going to do it.

1. Bypass mental defense programs so we can speak directly to the decision-making part of their minds.

2. Let them know that there are two available options, to join or not to join.

3. Remind our prospects of their reasons for listening to our presentation.

Here is an example.

"Which is going to be easier for you, to keep things the same and have nothing change, including finances, or to get started today, so that this time next year you can fire your boss and never have to go to work again?"

Did we speak directly to the decision-making part of the mind?

Yes. We started with the eight magic words, "Which is going to be easier for you…"

With this simple phrase of eight magic words, we have signalled to our prospects that there is more than one option that they can choose from. Both options are easy. All they need to do at this point is choose the easiest option.

Did we let the prospect know that there are two available options?

Yes, we have presented the two different options available, as well as explained the outcome they can expect from each of the two different choices.

What about our prospect's personal reason for listening to our presentation?

We have already informed our prospect that by joining us and getting started, our prospect can expect to get the outcome they are looking for. In the case of our example above, we said to our prospect, "… get started today, so that this time next year you can fire your boss and never have to go to work again?"

What do we do after our prospect chooses to get started?

Well, we can do one of four things.

- Invite the prospect to sign up now.
- Invite the prospect to meet up with us at a later date.

- Invite the prospect to meet up with someone in our upline.
- Invite the prospect to attend an event.

Whichever we choose to invite our prospects to do, we can relax and take it easy. The hard part of prospecting has been dealt with. They have already made a "yes" decision and that means we can comfortably invite them to take action and do any one of those four things without worry. We just need to choose the option that would work for our current situation.

So, there we have it.

Now, if you are ready to take everything we have learnt about prospecting in this book and put it all together, move on to the next chapter where we will do exactly that.

PUTTING EVERYTHING TOGETHER

By Jonathan Yap

LET'S REVIEW.

So, here is our formula for talking to prospects. The five steps are:

1. Rapport.

2. Icebreaker.

3. Decision.

4. Presentation.

5. Call to action.

Here is an example of how that would work in real life.

Let's say you are at a birthday party. An old friend walks up to you and says, "Hi! Haven't seen you in a long time. What have you been up to lately?"

Well, here is an example of what you might say to that.

You: Well, you know how most people feel that the world is getting more expensive?

Friend: Yes.

You: And most people would agree the cost of everything is going up, but not our salaries.

Friend: Now, that is very true! Especially when you have kids. In fact, the bulk of my salary every month goes to taking care of my children.

You: Well, I just found out how to make some extra cash every month without my boss knowing about it.

Friend: Really?

You: Yes. I am just curious; let's say you discovered how to make extra money every month. How much extra money would you be looking to make every month, and just out of curiosity, what would you do with that money?

Friend: If I could make an extra $500 a month, I would be so happy, as I could pay off some of my loan payments.

You: Wonderful! I can tell you everything you need to know in one minute. Do you have one minute now?

Friend: Yeah! Now would be good.

You: If you want to earn an extra $500 a month, you need to do these three things.

Number one. You know how when we find something we like, we want to tell everyone about it? Things like the best restaurant to eat at or the best place to take a holiday. Well, don't change. Continue to tell people about the things you like.

Number two. We have a juice that tastes amazing. Plus, it has all the vitamins and essential minerals our growing children need.

Number three. All you have to do is drink a little of our delicious juice with your children every morning. Then find five people who feel the same as you. People who want their children to be healthier and fall sick less often, and who would want to make some extra cash. Now, you don't have to find all five people right away. You can do it in a month, a year, or even take ten years. How fast or slow is entirely up to you.

Now, there may be one problem. Most people who are new to this business may not know how to find these five people or what to teach them once they find them. That is why we have an education system in place to show everybody, step-by-step, exactly what they need to do and how to do it.

Just like we learnt how to walk, talk, and read, we can learn how to earn an extra $500 a month.

That is all. And the rest is up to you.

So, what would you like to know next?

Friend: Is $500 the limit or can I earn more?

You: No, you can earn more than $500 a month. What would you like to know next?

Friend: Sounds good. I have no more questions.

You: So, which would be easier for you? To carry on with life the way it is or to get started so that you can start earning that extra $500 a month as soon as possible?

Friend: How do I get started?

You: Why don't we do this? Let's find a time to sit down with my friend, Tom. He has been doing this longer and has more experience than I do. So, he is someone you definitely want to meet with.

That was not too difficult, don't you think?

Will our formula work on people we just met?

So far in this book, we have learnt how to talk to people we already know. But what about strangers? Will our formula work on people we just met as well?

The answer is yes. Let me explain.

A very common and natural question among friends or relatives is, "What have you been doing lately?"

This question opens the door for us to transition from social chit-chat into business talk. And we can do so using the formula we have come up with in this book.

However, this is not a question that people who just met each other would ask. So, how then can we transition the conversation into business talk with people we just met?

We look for a different question, of course.

For people we just met, the question that will help us transition into business talk is, "What do you do for a living?"

Now, when someone asks us what we do for a living, that opens the door for us to use our formula. All we need to do is use a different sequence of magic words in front of our icebreaker. The words "I just found out" seem awkward and out of place when replying to the question, "What do you do for a living?"

So, we are going to use the words "I show people" instead.

Let's see how that works.

So, you are at a success seminar and during the break, the person next to you turns to you and both of you get into a small conversation. After saying hello and exchanging names, this person you just met asks you, "So, what is it you do for a living?"

Now, consider these two icebreakers.

1. I just found out how to make some extra cash every month without my boss knowing about it.

2. I show people how to make some extra cash every month without their boss knowing about it.

Did you notice how the first icebreaker seems awkward and out of place in response to the question, "What do you do for a living?"

The second icebreaker sounds a lot more natural and comfortable when we are telling people what it is that we do for a living, doesn't it?

There we have it.

Our formula is simple and can be used in conversations with friends, family, or strangers alike.

If you are ready for more examples, let's move on to the next chapter.

MORE EXAMPLES.

For health and nutrition.

Prospect: What do you do for a living?

You: Well, you know how most people say everything in life is getting more expensive?

Prospect: Yeah, you are right.

You: And most people would agree that everything is going up but not our salaries.

Prospect: That is very true.

You: Well, what I do is show people how to make some extra money every month without risking their current job.

Prospect: Really?

You: Yes. Can I ask you something?

Prospect: Go ahead.

You: Let's say you discovered how to make extra money every month; what would you do with that money?

Prospect: I would love to travel more.

You: Awesome! I am just curious, how much extra money would you need to make every month to make that happen?

Prospect: Maybe $1000.

You: Wonderful! I can tell you everything you need to know in one minute. Do you have one minute now?

Prospect: Yes.

You: If you want to earn an extra $1000 a month, you need to do these three things.

Number one. You know how when we find something we like, we want to tell everyone about it?

For example, the best place to take a holiday. Well, don't change. Continue to tell people about the things you like.

Number two. We are in the health and nutrition business, which means we have an amazing little pill that has all the vitamins and essential minerals we need to keep our immune system strong. After all, the last thing we want is to fall sick while we are on vacation, right?

Number three. All you have to do is take one little pill every morning. Then find five people who feel the same as you. People who want to be healthier, fall sick less often, and don't mind making some extra money every month. Now, you don't have to find all five people right away. You can do it in a month, a year, or even take ten years. How fast or slow is entirely up to you.

Now, there may be one problem. Most people who are new to this business may not know how to find these five people or what to teach them once they find them. That is why we have an education system in place to show everybody, step-by-step, exactly what they need to do and how to do it.

Just like we learnt how to walk, talk, and read, we can learn how to start a small business and earn an extra $1000 a month.

That is all. And the rest is up to you.

So, what would you like to know next?

Prospect: I don't have any questions.

You: So, which would be easier for you? To stay the same and have nothing change, or to get started now and hopefully by this time next year be making that extra $1000 every month?

Prospect: How do I get started?

You: Why don't we do this? Let's find a place to sit down and I'll show you how to fill out this online form which gets you started.

For skincare.

Prospect: What is your profession?

You: Well, you know how most people complain that their jobs don't pay enough?

Prospect: Yes.

You: And you know how most people would love to have more money in their lives?

Prospect: Yeah.

You: Well, what I do is show people how to start their own small business on a part-time basis and make some extra cash every month.

Prospect: Sounds interesting.

You: It gets better. Can I ask you something?

Prospect: Go ahead.

You: Let's say you discovered how to make extra money every month; how much extra money are you looking to make every month?

Prospect: If I could make an extra $1500 a month, I would be so happy.

You: That is good. I am just curious, what would you do with that money?

Prospect: Use that money for my children, of course.

You: Wonderful! I can tell you everything you need to know in one minute. Do you have one minute now?

Prospect: Yes.

You: If you want to earn an extra $1500 a month, you need to do these three things.

Number one. You know how when we find something we like, we want to tell everyone about it? Things like the best schools to put our children in or the best vacation spots to bring our kids to. Well, don't change. Continue to tell people about the things you like.

Number two. We have an amazing serum which gets rid of wrinkles and helps people look younger while they sleep.

Number three. All you have to do is use this serum every night before bed. Then find five people who feel the same as you. People who want to look younger and make some additional money every month. Now, you don't have to find all five people right away. You can do it in a month, a year, or even ten years. How fast or slow is entirely up to you.

Now, there may be one problem. Most people who are new to this business may not know how to find these five people or what to teach them once they find them. That is why we have an education system in place to show everybody, step-by-step, exactly what they need to do and how to do it.

Just like we learnt how to walk, talk, and read, we can learn how to earn an extra $1500 a month through a small part-time business.

That is all. And the rest is up to you.

So, what would you like to know next?

Prospect: You only have a serum? What about other products?

You: No, we have an entire range of skincare products. Which ones you choose to use and talk about is entirely up to you.

Prospect: Sounds good.

You: So, which would be easier for you? To stay the same and have nothing change or to get started now, so that by this time next year, you will not only be looking younger but will also be making that extra $1500 every month?

Prospect: Looks like I have to get started.

You: Well, why don't you come on down this Saturday? I'm getting some friends together to chat more about this over coffee. I'll show you exactly how to get started then.

For travel.

Prospect: Do you work or are you still studying?

You: I have a business. Well, you know how it is hard for most people to get a raise nowadays?

Prospect: Yeah, you are right.

You: And with the cost of everything going up, most people would agree that extra income every month would be useful.

Prospect: That is very true.

You: Well, what I do is show people how to make some extra income every month, so they don't have to worry about not getting a raise ever again.

Prospect: How do you do that?

You: Can I ask you something?

Prospect: Go ahead.

You: I am just curious, how much extra monthly income are you looking for?

Prospect: $500 would be nice.

You: Just out of curiosity, what would happen if you made that $500 every month?

Prospect: I could pay off some of my bills.

You: Cool! I can tell you everything you need to know in one minute. Do you have one minute now?

Prospect: Yeah! Now would be good.

You: If you want to earn an extra $500 a month to pay off your bills, you need to do these three things.

Number one. You know how when we find something we like, we want to tell everyone about it? Things like the best restaurant to eat at or the best place to take a holiday. Well, don't change. Continue to tell people about the things you like.

Number two. We are in the travel discount business. That means we help people get the best discounts possible on things like their hotels and air tickets.

Number three. All you have to do is start paying less for your vacations. Then find five people who feel the same as you. People who want to pay less when they travel, and who want to make some extra income. Now, you don't have to find all five people right away. You can do it in a month, a year, or even ten years. How fast or slow is entirely up to you.

Now, there may be one problem. Most people who are new to this business may not know how to find these five people or what to teach them once they find them. That is why we have an education system in place to show everybody, step-by-step, exactly what they need to do and how to do it.

Just like we learnt how to walk, talk, and read, we can learn how to earn an extra $500 a month.

That is all. And the rest is up to you.

So, what would you like to know next?

Prospect: Sounds good. How do I get started?

You: Let's find a place to sit down and I'll show you how to fill out this online form which gets you started.

For essential oils.

Prospect: What have you been up to lately?

You: Well, you know how most people complain that the money from their job is not enough?

Prospect: Yeah.

You: And have you noticed that most people would love to make more money on the side if it didn't affect their current job?

Prospect: True.

You: Well, I just found out how to make some extra cash every month without quitting our current job.

Prospect: Really?

You: Yes. Can I ask you something?

Prospect: Go ahead.

You: How much extra money are you looking to make every month? And what would you do with that money?

Prospect: If I could make an extra $2000 a month, I would be so happy as I could pay off all my bills and still have some left over.

You: Wonderful! I can tell you everything you need to know in one minute. Do you have one minute now?

Prospect: Yes.

You: If you want to earn an extra $2000 a month to pay off all your bills, you need to do these three things.

Number one. You know how when we find something we like, we want to tell everyone about it? Things like the best street food to eat or the best hangout spots. Well, don't change. Continue to tell people about the things you like.

Number two. We have a special oil that helps people with their stress.

Number three. All you have to do is whenever you feel stress, especially at work, just rub two drops of our oil between your palms and then take slow deep breaths to inhale the aroma. You will feel the stress start to melt away almost immediately. Then find three people who feel the same as you. People who want less stress in their lives and want to make some extra cash.

Now, you don't have to find all three people right away. You can do it in a month, a year, or even ten years. How fast or slow is entirely up to you.

Now, there may be one problem. Most people who are new to this business may not know how to find these three people or what to teach them once they find them. That is why we have an education system in place to show everybody, step-by-step, exactly what they need to do and how to do it.

Just like we learnt how to walk, talk, and read, we can learn how to earn an extra $2000 a month.

That is all. And the rest is up to you.

So, what would you like to know next?

Prospect: Sounds good to me.

You: So, which would be easier for you? To stay the same and have nothing change or to get started now and hopefully by this time next year you will be making that extra $2000 every month?

Prospect: How do I get started?

You: Why don't you come up to my place this Sunday? A few of my friends are getting together during tea-time. You can experience our stress-relieving oil and I'll show you how to get started.

IS IT REALLY THAT EASY?

Now, the question on most people's minds reading this for the first time is normally, "Is it really so easy? We just use our formula and people want to join immediately?"

Remember what we talked about earlier in this book?

We are not here to manipulate or pressure anyone into becoming a customer or distributor. We just deliver our message to the decision-making part of our prospects' minds and leave the decision up to them.

At the end of our business talk, our prospects can make one of three choices:

Choice #1: I want to do business with you.

Choice #2: I don't want to do business with you.

Choice #3: I have a question.

Our job here is easy.

If a prospect chooses Choice #1, then our job is easy. All we need to do next is guide them through the sign-up process.

If a prospect chooses Choice #2, no problem. All we need to do is start talking about other topics and have a pleasant social conversation.

If a prospect has a question, which is Choice #3, then all we need to do is answer their question and check again to see if they want to join or not.

Answering questions is easy.

Remember, we are not here to manipulate or pressure our prospects into joining. Our job is to deliver our message to the decision-making part of their minds and leave the decision entirely up to them.

With that in mind, answering questions becomes easy for us because all we need to do is to answer their questions as honestly as we know how to.

Our prospects can then decide what is best for them. If their decision is "no" after hearing our answer, it is okay.

We have done our job and we can move on to the next prospect.

Can we improve?

Definitely. As we gain more experience, naturally we will get better at answering questions. But for now, especially if you are new in network marketing, being honest is the best approach.

THE REST IS UP TO YOU.

There are four types of people in this world.

The first type is closed-minded people. These people have their minds already made up that the techniques and strategies shared within this book will not work, even before they start reading. They tell themselves things like:

- "I've read a lot of books and they are all the same."
- "This will not work in my country."

Needless to say, this type of person will not gain anything from this book.

The second type of people are the passive readers. They have read through this book, but they will never put the skills and techniques into action. So, this book has been nothing more than entertainment to them.

The third type of people are the people who will take action and give the techniques in this book a try. However, the people in this group lack commitment and they give up easily. This type of person will also not gain much from this book.

Then we have the fourth type of people, those who read this book with 100% commitment. This means that they don't only glance through the book once. Instead, they will read and re-read this book over and over again to internalise the concepts and techniques. Furthermore, they take action and put the techniques into practice. These people are the ones who create significant change in the results they generate in their network marketing businesses.

To gain the most from this book, I encourage you to read this book with 100% commitment and most importantly, put the skills and techniques you learn in this book into practice.

Have fun prospecting!

ABOUT THE AUTHOR

Over the last 17 years, Jonathan Yap has pioneered and supported network marketing not only in Singapore, but Cambodia, Philippines, and other southeast Asian countries. He leads the Network Marketing Questions group on Facebook, dedicated to helping all network marketers improve their skills.

Printed in Great Britain
by Amazon

34552497R00076